KENTUCKY

A Turner Educational Services, Inc. book. Based on the Portrait
of America television series created by R.E. (Ted) Turner.

Library of Congress Number: 86-17740

1234567890   9089888786

Library of Congress Cataloging in Publication Data

Thompson, Kathleen.
  Kentucky.

  (Portrait of America)
  "A Turner book."
  Summary: Discusses the history, economy, culture,
and future of Kentucky. Also includes a state
chronology, pertinent statistics, and maps.
    1. Kentucky—Juvenile literature. [1. Kentucky]
I. Title. II. Series: Thompson, Kathleen.
Portrait of America.
F451.3.T48   1986   976.9   86-17740
ISBN 0-86514-453-2 (lib. bdg.)
ISBN 0-86514-528-8 (softcover)

Cover Photo: Bill Straus

★ ★ ★ ★
Portrait of AMERICA

KENTUCKY

Kathleen Thompson

A TURNER BOOK
RAINTREE PUBLISHERS

Covington

Ashland

Louisville

FRANKFORT

Owensboro

Lexington

Paducah

Bowling Green

Elkton

CONTENTS

Introduction

Kentucky, the Bluegrass State.

"They always say you can't go home again. . . . You can go home again, and I've done it. And I love it here."

Kentucky: coal, mountains, thoroughbreds, industry, Bluegrass music.

"Kentucky has everything that I'm looking for in life, and I don't have any desire really to move or go anywhere else."

Once a great Indian hunting ground, Kentucky has moved through the hardships of the pioneers and the coal miners. Today Kentucky is a vital state, filled with natural beauty and colored by a fascinating culture. It is as lively as the music of a Bluegrass fiddler.

The Kentucky Derby is held each May in Louisville.

The Hunting Ground

Once the land we call Kentucky was part of a great hunting ground. The towering trees of its forests, the lush undergrowth, the crystal streams were home, not for any human beings, but for animals, birds, and fish.

Surrounding the hunting ground were the settlements of five tribes—the Cherokee, Chickasaw, Wyandot, Delaware, and Shawnee. There was an agreement among the tribes not to move in and disturb the forests. Instead, their hunters made trips along the Warriors' Path that went from Cumberland Gap to the Ohio River. They brought back to their tribes the game that was needed for food and furs.

It was an arrangement that led to peace and prosperity for these tribes. But it was one that the white man, when he

"Before the White Man Came," showing members of a peaceful Indian tribe, was painted by C.M. Russell.

came, would not understand.

The first Europeans who came into the area left it untouched. They probably included the English explorers Abram Wood, Gabriel Arthur, and John Peter Salley and the French explorers Jacques Marquette, Louis Joliet, and Sieur de la Salle. Then in 1750, Dr. Thomas Walker passed through the Cumberland Gap, which he named. He went as far as the Cumberland River before returning to Virginia with stories of the richness and beauty of the land.

It was in the year 1767 that Daniel Boone made his first trip to Kentucky. Two years later he came back with a group of hunters. Many times the Indians found Boone and his men in the hunting ground. Again and again they took away the furs Boone's group had gathered and escorted them politely out of the area. Again and again Boone came back.

To Daniel Boone and the other white men who saw Kentucky, it seemed like unclaimed land. No-one lived on it. No one owned it. In 1773, Boone brought a group of settlers into Kentucky. But the Indians made them turn

Above is Daniel Boone. On the right-hand page is an etching by Alfred Jones called "Daniel Boone and His Companions Discovering Kentucky".

around and go back.

A year later, the northwest Indians lost an important battle with soldiers from Virginia. They had to sign a treaty giving up their rights to all land south of the Ohio River. That included the hunting ground. In the same year, James Harrod founded the first permanent white settlement in Kentucky.

The next year, the Cherokee sold their rights in the area to the Transylvania Company and

Daniel Boone founded Boonesboro on the south bank of the Kentucky River.

But there were still Indians who had not lost or sold the rights to their hunting grounds. They no longer tried to lead the white man peacefully out of their land. Now they began to fight.

In 1776, Kentucky became part of Virginia's Fincastle County. Late that year, the area became Kentucky County. During the Revolutionary War, separated from the other colonies by high mountains and dense forests, the Kentucky settlers had to defend themselves against Indian attacks. There was little help from outside. Daniel Boone, Simon Kenton, and George Rogers Clark led the Indian fighters.

In 1778, Clark led more than a thousand men against the Indian, French, and British at Kaskaskia, Cahokia, and Vincennes. Four years later, the Indians defeated the settlers at Blue Licks.

The State House in Frankfort was built in 1795 and burned in 1813.

But this was the last major battle between Indians and white settlers in Kentucky.

Because they had received so little help in their fights from the other colonies, a feeling was growing in Kentucky that they ought to be independent. So in 1784, the settlers held a convention at Danville to consider separating from Virginia. There were nine of these conventions before Kentucky decided to become a state of the Union rather than an independent country.

In 1792, Kentucky became the fifteenth state. In the years that followed, more land was opened to settlement. The population grew. Horse breeding began in central Kentucky. On hemp, tobacco, and cotton farms, slave labor was used, but in 1833 the state passed a law that no more slaves could be brought in.

When the Civil War came, Kentucky was bitterly divided.

Workers spreading hemp on a Kentucky farm.

The state tried to remain neutral, but it was invaded by both sides. More than seventy thousand men from Kentucky fought for the Union. More than thirty thousand fought for the Confederacy. The presidents of both sides were men born in Kentucky.

It was only after the war that Kentucky became strongly sympathetic to the South. Some of the laws passed during what is called Reconstruction were unwise and some of them were downright unfair to the South. Kentucky suffered from them and developed stronger ties to its southern neighbors.

The railroads boosted Kentucky's economy in the late 1800s. Above a rail shipment by the Procter Coal Company crosses a trestle.

Kentucky also suffered from the economic depression that hit the South after the war. Many tobacco farmers went bankrupt. Farmers banded together in groups to fight for laws that would help them. Meanwhile, industry was recovering rapidly.

Things got better for Kentucky in the last part of the century. For one thing, the railroads had come into their own. Now, Kentucky products could be shipped to areas that could afford them. Timber and coal and racehorses also began to bring back Kentucky's prosperity.

At the turn of the century, something terrible happened in Kentucky politics. The race for

William Taylor

William Goebel

governor in 1899 was a hot one. Feelings ran high on both sides. When the votes were counted, Republican William S. Taylor seemed to have won. But it was so close that his Democratic opponent, William Goebel, demanded a recount.

And then before a final decision was made, Goebel was shot. As he lay dying, the general assembly declared him governor. On his death, his lieutenant governor, J.C.W. Beckham, took office.

Taylor and his followers did not accept this. They set up a rival government. It looked as though Kentucky was headed for civil war. Finally, the U.S. Supreme Court declared Beckham the rightful governor. But the two political parties remained bitterly opposed for many years.

At about this same time, a small group of tobacco companies

banded together to buy all the tobacco grown in Kentucky. That way they weren't competing with each other, and they could pay the farmers very low prices. Eventually the farmers fought back. During the Black Patch War, which lasted from 1904 to 1909, farmers rode out into the night burning the fields, barns, and warehouses of growers who sold to the monopoly. The result was that the group broke up and tobacco auctions were used to sell the farmers' crops.

That improved things for tobacco farmers. But otherwise things were again very bad in Kentucky economically. During the Great Depression, small farms could not survive. Miners were thrown out of work. People survived by taking jobs on government projects—building highways and factories, working to create state and national parks, building Fort Knox.

World War II brought a real

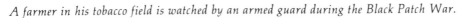

A farmer in his tobacco field is watched by an armed guard during the Black Patch War.

A coal mine once operated by the Procter Coal Company.

boom in manufacturing. It also reopened the mines and brought life back to many of Kentucky's farms. But new farming methods meant that small farms began to be combined into larger ones. Many farmers went to work in manufacturing or in the growing tourist industry. By 1970 most of the population of Kentucky lived in cities.

During the late 1960s, Kentucky faced many of the changes in race relations that were found in the rest of the country. An open housing law was passed and public employment and public facilities were opened to blacks. In the 1970s school busing met with considerable opposition.

Also in the 1970s, the coal mining industry boomed because of the energy shortage. And Kentucky was the country's leading producer of coal.

Kentucky has come a long way from the days of the Indian hunting ground. And yet the startling beauty of mountains and forests can still be found here. It has also come a long way from the days of the pioneers. But their spirit lives in Kentucky's people.

One Family's Courage

"In the late twenties, when they were really trying to crack my dad, destroy him, I suffered a lot of indignities, even from black kids where I went to school. . . . I was pushed around, shoved around, called nasty names, knocked down. I

John Nation

had one experience where my dad was supporting a Democrat for mayor and someone rode by our house and fired a shot through a window. The bullet lodged about four or five feet above my head in the bed where I was sleeping. Wasn't a very pleasant time."

Woodford Porter's father was a man of vision. He believed that black votes could mean something. He also believed that the Democratic Party would work harder and do more for the black people than the Republican Party. But the Republican Party was the party of Abraham Lincoln, so Porter had to fight not only whites but also his black neighbors. Still he raised his son Woodford to believe in the vote.

"Involvement in politics is the best way in order to find better ways, better avenues for your people. Everyone talks about black political power, and there certainly is power in politics. There's power in votes."

The Porter family business is a mortuary that serves the black community. That business has given Woodford Porter a certain amount of independence. He has not had to worry about losing business because he took unpopular stands.

On the left-hand page are Woodford Porter, Sr. and Woodford Porter, Jr. Above is A.D. Porter.

By the time the civil rights movement became strong in Kentucky, there was another generation of Porters around to stand up for what they believed.

"It seemed to have been a race in my house to see who was going to get arrested the most times, in a way. But I said, do whatever your conscience dic-

tates. I'll support you. So they got arrested a few times. One time they got arrested and hadn't had dinner. They wouldn't serve them dinner. . . . Well, I bought I think eighty dollars worth of White Castle hamburgers to feed them that evening."

Alongside their political struggles, the Porters have always carried on their financial enterprises. Today, Ferda Porter is breaking new ground. She has opened an office supply store—downtown.

"I think Ferda's pioneering is far more exiciting and far more interesting because she's going after a market that every other businessman in the United States is going after. And Ferda's market is a market that is not circumscribed by race or class or anything."

The Porters are a remarkable family. And one of the most remarkable things about them is the strength and love they give to each other. You can hear it in Ferda Porter's words when she talks about her father.

"He's always there and I know I can count on him to help me. And help doesn't mean doing for all the time. Help just sometimes means, you know, knowing that that hand is there. Reach out and grab it if you need it."

The Porters outside their family-run funeral home.

The Tie That Binds

"A family in the Kentucky mountains, especially in eastern Kentucky, means your clan. And our family is now scattered all over the country. But still, if ever there's a call that goes out and says, 'We're going to get together,' everybody'll break their necks to get here."

The Ritchie family is indeed scattered all over the country. But they're still connected. Some of the little Ritchies don't look exactly like the ones that went before. Their hair is a little curlier, their eyes a different shape, their skin a different color. But they all come back to the home place when it's time for a reunion.

Jean Ritchie is a famous folksinger who lives in New York now. But she remembers some of the things that made the family so close.

"Our family lived down here at the mouth of the creek. Well, we could see Aunt Maggie's house through the trees. Many times a family lived out of sight of the next house and it was a little community all to itself. . . . I know we could have a party just with ourselves if Mom took a notion to make some pull candy or something like that. She'd just

make up a batch of candy and fudge or something and we'd all get out there and dance and play music and have our own family party."

When a family starts with ties that close, they don't disappear. Distance may stretch them thin, but they remain strong, strong enough to bring people back to the hills. They may even be valued more from a little way off. Amanda Coffey feels that way.

"We're from Atlanta, really, right now. But after we got away a while from the mountains, being a hillbilly meant more and we're, we're proud of it. You could've called us that back when we lived here and we would have been mad. We're not mad anymore. We're very proud of it."

Proud of the family. Proud of its values. Proud of their home. That pride is part of what it means to be from Kentucky. It's what brings Jean Ritchie back.

"They always say you can't go home again. Somebody wrote that down in a book and everybody seems to think that that makes it absolutely true. But it's not. You can go home again, and I've done it. And I love it here. I've traveled all around the world, but I still love this place better than any other."

A Sunday morning Ritchie family reunion at Graveyard Memorial. In the foreground is Jean Ritchie.

Photos by George Pickow

Bluegrass Business

There are a lot of different kinds of land in Kentucky. There is fertile farmland. There are coal-rich mountains. There are forests, and there are grassy meadows. And the economy of the state is as varied as its land. Kentucky is one of the few states in the Union that has important manufacturing, agricultural, mining, and tourist industries.

Economically, Kentucky's biggest problem is that, while the economy is growing, there are still too many people who have very low incomes. In Appalachia, the average 1980 family income was less than $6,000 a year. But that was up almost $2,000 from the 1976 figure. Things are changing in Kentucky.

Manufacturing is the leading economic activity. It began to edge out farming right after the Civil War and has been

Photos courtesy General Motors

growing ever since. Manufacturing accounts for almost $11 billion in income every year in Kentucky.

The largest area of manufacturing is nonelectric machinery. That category covers a lot of ground. In Kentucky it includes air conditioning and heating equipment, typewriters, tractors, conveyors, and ball bearings. Factories in Kentucky also make machinery that helps to control air pollution.

Next in importance is transportation equipment. The state that once raised horses to carry pioneers over the countryside now builds automobiles to take commuters to work. Instead of workhorses, Kentucky now produces trucks and also railroad equipment.

The third largest area of manufacturing is electrical machinery and equipment. Your household appliances—toasters, blenders, electric can openers—may very

On the left-hand page, a new Corvette comes off the assembly line.

Below: a Corvette welding operation (left) and a nearly-completed Corvette body (right).

well come from a Kentucky factory. Kentucky factories also make electrical and electronic controls and electric motors.

Food products are an important source of income in Kentucky. The largest single part of this industry, however, manufactures something that hardly qualifies as a food. Kentucky is the country's largest producer of bourbon whiskey. Kentuckians also make bakery goods, meat products, and soft drinks.

Another area of manufacturing is closely linked to agriculture in Kentucky. The fifth largest manufacturing activity in Kentucky is making tobacco products.

Coal makes mining second only to manufacturing in the economy of Kentucky. No other state produces as much coal as Kentucky.

But coal is not the state's only valuable mineral. Petroleum is produced in the same parts of the state that produce coal—the Western Coal Field and the Appalachian Plateau. Limestone and natural gas also add to the importance of mining in the state's economy.

Agriculture remains a significant part of life in Kentucky. The economy no longer depends, as it did before the Civil War, on tobacco farming. But tobacco is still the state's largest cash crop. Kentucky is the second-ranked tobacco growing state. Other farm crops include soybeans, corn, and wheat as well as apples and popcorn.

Maker's Mark Distillery

A worker seals a bottle of Maker's Mark Whisky at left.

28

Kentucky is famous for its horses (above) and its tobacco (below).

In Kentucky when you talk about livestock, you're talking about horses. Kentucky has always been famous for breeding horses. Today, the horses are thoroughbreds, primarily used in racing.

Horses are not the only animals raised on Kentucky farms. Beef cattle bring in almost as much income as horses. Dairy products, hogs, eggs, and young chickens are also important agricultural products.

Still, it's hard to think about Kentucky without thinking about elegant thoroughbred horses grazing quietly on Kentucky Bluegrass.

29

Horse Sense

"I was born in the horse business. I really had more interest in that than I ever did in going to school. That's all I was ever interested in."

You just can't talk about Kentucky without talking about horses. From the Bluegrass farms where they're raised to the Kentucky Derby where they're raced, if you're looking for horses, you'll find them here.

The Taylor family is right there in the middle of the horse business. Joe Taylor is farm manager at Gainesway, one of the top horse farms in the world. His sons have fulfilled a long time dream of his and created their own farm. It's called Taylormade.

"We knew we wanted to be in the horse business. We always knew that. Because that's the business he'd been in. We've always wanted to please him and so we just followed in his footsteps, trying to do the best we can."

Below is the Taylormade Farm. On the right-hand page are the Taylors.

Photos courtesy Taylor Made Sales Agency

Taylor Made Sales Agency

The best the Taylor boys can do is pretty good. They started by boarding a few mares. Now they're building a reputation as a sales agency for thoroughbred yearlings. But horses are more than a business for the Taylors. Joe Taylor puts it this way.

"The horse is my favorite animal. I don't dislike a dog or a cat. But I think a horse shows enough emotion that I just like to be around them. They're thankful for what you do for them."

His son Mark puts it another way.

"You know, it just depends on the horse. And horses are just like people. Some of them you don't like, some of them you do."

On the left-hand page is Mark Taylor leading Rosemont Risk against the background of an exciting Kentucky Derby race.

The Art of the Country

As the United States grew from a small collection of colonies to a vast nation that filled half of the North American continent, a strange thing happened. A group of people in the Appalachian Mountains lived in a world apart. There were few roads leading in. The country around them was rugged and hard to cross. Hardly anyone ever went in or out of Kentucky's eastern mountains.

And so the people of Appalachia did not become part of the melting pot. They continued to sing the songs their ancestors brought with them from England, songs from the time of Shakespeare. They told the folktales and made the crafts of a time that was being forgotten by the rest of the country.

Roads were finally built into Appalachia in the 1920s. But

Kentucky is rich in arts and craftwork. Shown here freshly dyed wool that has been hung to dry in trees.

the culture of this mountain region still gives Kentucky a special quality.

There's another side to Kentucky culture. Outside the mountains, the people developed strong ties to the plantation life of the South. One of America's great southern writers lived and wrote in Kentucky.

Robert Penn Warren won the Pulitzer Prize three times. His best-known novel, *All the King's Men,* was based on the life of Louisiana governor Huey Long.

Then of course, there is Bluegrass music. The fiddles sing. The banjos dazzle. It's music for dancing—if your feet can move that fast.

In Louisville, you will find an outstanding symphony orchestra, a ballet troupe, an excellent art museum, and one of the most outstanding theaters in the country.

The Actors Theater of Louisville became Kentucky's state theater in 1974. Every year people from all over the country come here to see fine productions of new plays that have

been chosen in one of the most important playwriting competitions in the world.

Because Kentucky honors the simplicity of its folk arts, some people have the wrong idea of life in this rich and varied culture. But it's a mistake to underestimate Kentucky—its art or its people.

A Bluegrass band performs below. On the right-hand page ballet dancers are pictured against the Louisville skyline.

King of the Courts

"They insinuated that they were professionals and we weren't. And I'm not saying that we are professional, but we can play croquet with anybody."

Archie Burchfield is a Kentucky tobacco farmer. He's a man who feels right at home with a hoe in his hand. But somewhere along the line he got comfortable with something else—a croquet mallet.

Lots of people started playing clay court croquet in Kentucky during the Depression. But if you think of croquet as a game that's played on the rolling lawn of an elegant mansion by men in white suits and women in graceful summer dresses—well, that's not the way they do it in Kentucky. That's not the way Archie Burchfield does it.

When Archie entered the National Tournament of the United States Croquet Association, he wasn't exactly welcomed with open arms.

"I mean we were invited, but to say we were 'received' . . . I'd say we weren't. But after we won the national tournament, well, we were received better."

Below is national croquet champion Archie Burchfield with his wife, Betty. On the right-hand page is Archie Burchfield against an autumn view of the Cumberland Gap.

Now Archie travels all over the country with his wife, Betty, competing in croquet tournaments in New York and Arizona and a lot of other places that are far from his old Kentucky home.

"New York's unbelievable to us. We're from a small community. We went to a cocktail party last night . . . on Park Avenue. Beautiful house and chandeliers about as big as my living room."

Archie may seem a little out of place at a cocktail party on Park Avenue, but his skill has made a place for him on the court. He's a good player and a tough one. And he loves the game.

"Croquet's a fascinating game. You can't start to grasp it if you're coming to see it the first time. Players that have been playing as long as I have here in the state—we know what we'll make you do seven shots, probably, ahead. So it's more like a chess game. I mean, we'll go to this corner. You might not know why we're going there. But three shots later you'll say, 'Uh oh. I know why he went there now.'"

It's that kind of know-how that makes Archie Burchfield a hard man to beat on the croquet court. If he doesn't dress or talk like everybody else, that doesn't bother him.

"Well, I don't aim to make them uncomfortable. I'm just myself. . . . I play all the time with my shirt out. . . . We just aim to play comfortable and enjoy it. That's all."

At the left, Archie Burchfield prepares for a shot. On the right-hand page, Archie gives some pointers to his son, Mark.

Courtesy Archie Burchfield

40

41

Taking Care of the Family— and the Future

Kentucky is a place of great beauty and rich natural resources. There is wealth in the soil and under it. Yet one of Kentucky's greatest challenges for the future is to provide more of its people with what they need for a good life.

The Appalachian Region has been, for too many years, dependent on the coal-mining industry. For a long time, there were jobs to be had in the mines, but they were dangerous and low paying. Today, machines have made the jobs less dangerous. And although the pay is much better, there are fewer jobs available. If poverty is to be wiped out in Appalachia, there will have to be new industries, new sources of income for the people.

The other group of Kentuckians for whom the future is

A strip coal mine of today.

uncertain is made up of farmers. More and more, farming is being replaced by "agribusiness." Large grain, soybean, and livestock producers are more in evidence today than small tobacco farmers. For the farmers, too, there are going to have to be new sources of income.

These are some of the people in the Kentucky family who will need help if they are going to stay here—at home. And yet, there is little doubt that they will stay. Kentucky seems to be a hard place to leave.

There is every reason to believe that Kentucky will meet the challenge of its future. The Cherokee called this beautiful place *Ken-ta-keh.* It meant "tomorrow." And tomorrow still has a special meaning in the state called Kentucky.

The Louisville Galleria.

Important Historical Events in Kentucky

1700s Kentucky is a hunting ground for the Cherokee, Chickasaw, Wyandot, Delaware, and the Shawnee.

1750 Dr. Thomas Walker explores the area and names the Cumberland Gap.

1767 Daniel Boone makes his first trip into Kentucky.

1773 Boone tries to bring in a group of settlers. They are turned back by Indians.

1774 The northwest Indians lose their rights to all land south of the Ohio River to Virginia. James Harrod founds the first permanent white settlement in Kentucky.

1775 The Cherokee sell their rights in the area to the Transylvania Company.

1776 Kentucky becomes part of Fincastle County of Virginia and then becomes Kentucky County.

1778 George Rogers Clark defeats French, Indians, and British at Kaskaskia, Cahokia, and Vincennes.

1782 The Indians defeat the settlers at Blue Licks in the last major battle between Indians and white settlers in Kentucky.

1784 The settlers hold the first of nine conventions to consider separating from Virginia.

1792 Kentucky becomes the fifteenth state.

1833 Kentucky passes a law that states that no more slaves can be brought in.

1861 The Civil War begins and Kentucky attempts to remain neutral.

1899 William Goebel, candidate for governor, is shot.

1904 The Black Patch War begins.

1936 Fort Knox is opened.

1970s The coal industry booms because of the energy shortage.

Kentucky Almanac

Nickname. The Bluegrass State.

Capital. Frankfort.

State Bird. Cardinal.

State Flower. Goldenrod.

State Tree. Kentucky coffee tree.

State Motto. United We Stand, Divided We Fall.

State Song. My Old Kentucky Home.

State Abbreviations. Ky. or Ken. (traditional); KY (postal).

Statehood. June 1, 1792, the 15th state.

Government. Congress: U.S. senators, 2; U.S. representatives, 7. **State Legislature:** senators, 38; representatives, 100. **Counties:** 120.

Area. 40,395 sq. mi. (104,623 sq. km.), 37th in size among the states.

Greatest Distances. north/south, 175 mi. (282 km.); east/west, 350 mi. (563 km.).

Elevation. Highest: Black Mountain, 4,145 ft. (1,263 m). **Lowest:** 257 ft. (78 m).

Population. 1980 Census: 3,661,433 (10% increase over 1970), 23rd in size among the states. **Density:** 90 persons per sq. mi. (35 persons per sq. km.). **Distribution:** 51% urban, 49% rural. **1970 Census:** 3,320,711.

Economy. Agriculture: tobacco, soybeans, corn, beef cattle, chickens. **Manufacturing:** nonelectrical machinery, primary metals, electrical and electronic products, food products, fabricated metal products, chemical products, printed materials. **Mining:** coal, crushed stone, petroleum, aluminum.

Places to Visit

Breaks of the Sandy, near Elkhorn City.
Elizabethtown.
Horse Farms, in the Lexington area.
Liberty Hall in Frankfort.
My Old Kentucky Home, near Bardstown.
Shakertown, near Lexington.

Annual Events

Lincoln Day Celebration in Hodgenville (February).
Kentucky Derby in Louisville (May).
Capital Expo in Frankfort (June).
Bluegrass Festival of the United States in Louisville (June).
State Fair in Louisville (August).
Kentucky Highland Folk Festival in Prestonburg (September).

Kentucky Counties

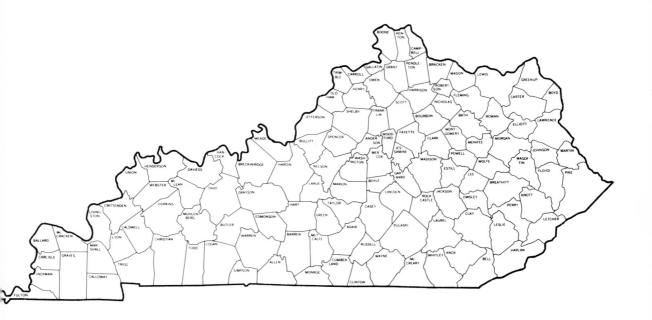

47

INDEX